Set design by Anna Louizos

Photo by Carol Rosegg

Ari Graynor and Alicia Silverstone in a scene from the Broadway production of *The Performers*.

THE PERFORMERS

BY DAVID WEST READ

★

★

DRAMATISTS
PLAY SERVICE
INC.

THE PERFORMERS
Copyright © 2013, David West Read

SPECIAL NOTE

Originally commissioned by South Coast Repertory.

Original Broadway production produced by
Robyn Goodman   Amanda Lipitz   Scott M. Delman
Cynthia Stroum   Playing Pretend Productions
Kevin Kinsella   Bruce Bendell/Scott Prisand
Morris Berchard   Richard Vague   Karen Segal   Russell J. Notides
Burnt Umber/Rebecca Gold   Debbie Buslik/Jamie Bendell
Kevin McCollum

SPECIAL NOTE ON SONGS AND RECORDINGS

*With thanks to my collaborator and friend, Evan Cabnet —
the hardest-working man in the business.*

THE PERFORMERS was produced on Broadway at the Longacre Theatre, opening on November 14, 2012. It was directed by Evan Cabnet; the scenic design was by Anna Louizos; the costume design was by Jessica Wegener-Shay; the lighting design was by Jeff Croiter; the sound design was by Nevin Steinberg; the projection design was by Richard DiBella; the hair and wig design were by Charles G. LaPointe; the prosthetics and make-up design were by Adam Bailey; the production stage manager was Charles M. Turner, III; and the stage manager was Matt Schreiber. The cast was as follows:

MANDREW .... Cheyenne Jackson
LEE .... Daniel Breaker
PEEPS .... Ari Graynor
SARA .... Alicia Silverstone
CHUCK .... Henry Winkler
SUNDOWN .... Jenni Barber

THE PERFORMERS

MANDREW — A male porn star in his late twenties.

LEE — Mandrew's friend, a journalist, late twenties.

PEEPS — Mandrew's wife, another porn star, mid-twenties.

SARA — Lee's fiancée, a high-school teacher, late twenties.

CHUCK — An aging male porn star, fifties to sixties.

SUNDOWN — Another female porn star, mid-twenties.

TIME

The present.

PLACE

A hotel in Las Vegas, Nevada.

THE PERFORMERS

Scene 1

A hotel room in Las Vegas. Late afternoon.

Mandrew (late 20s) stalks around the room in costume — a brown caveman-style wrap, tied at the shoulder. He's in good shape, comfortable with his body, and he's getting ready for a party.

Lee (late 20s), more conservatively dressed, sits with his notepad and pen in hand.

MANDREW. What is a porn star? Good question. That's the first good question you've asked all day.
LEE. I didn't actually ask that question —
MANDREW. A porn star is someone who excites you sexually but not emotionally. Ipso facto, I'm not a porn star, I am a love star, I make *love*.
LEE. Does anyone call you a love star?
MANDREW. No, nobody *calls* me that, obviously. They call me Mandrew. That's my name, so ...
LEE. It is *now*. I'm still getting used to it.
MANDREW. Just because something excites you — write this down — just because something excites you ... doesn't mean it's porn. I used to jack off to *Where's Waldo* books. There, I said it.
LEE. You used to masturbate to *Where's Waldo* books?
MANDREW. Constantly. I used to get so hard, just looking for Waldo in all those crowded places ... never knowing when he was gonna pop up ... it's the thrill of the chase, man! As soon as I'd find that fucker I'd whip it out and BOOM! Cum all over his striped little cap.

LEE. Okay. Well that's fascinating, but I can't really print that, so …

MANDREW. Oh, I'm sorry, that's not appropriate for the *New York Times?*

LEE. It's the *New York Post.*

MANDREW. Whatever. I feel like I'm in the dark over here, and meanwhile *you're* the one who hasn't done your research — writing an article for the *New York* whatever and you haven't even watched my film.

LEE. The article's not focusing on the films. It's about you, and what it's like to be a performer.

MANDREW. What are you calling it?

LEE. Doesn't matter what I'm calling it …

MANDREW. Come on, what's the title?

LEE. "P-star Makes It Big."

MANDREW. *(Beat.)* That's really good.

LEE. Thank you.

MANDREW. You know what's *not* a good title? *Planet of the Tits.* Fingers, the director …

LEE. The director's name is "Fingers"?

MANDREW. Yeah, I mean his real name is Charles Fingerbang, but everyone calls him "Fingers."

LEE. Let me just write that down …

MANDREW. The guy's a genius, you should check out his shit, if the *New York Times* is interested in seeing some art for a change —

LEE. *New York Post* —

MANDREW. His titles are shit, but he's basically like the Martin Scorsese of porn.

LEE. Right, so what kind of direction does he give you?

MANDREW. Well, so this scene that I'm nominated for, I'm goin' down on this chick — you know Sundown LeMay? She's got an ass that goes boom boom boom, all the way around.

LEE. I've seen her work.

MANDREW. Yeah, so I'm going down on her and she's lovin' it, obviously, and this other chick's just watching, so as an actor I'm thinking in my head like maybe she's my cousin Amanda or something.

LEE. What?

MANDREW. No, you know what I mean. Like it's forbidden, as a backstory.

LEE. That's kind of weird.

MANDREW. It's not weird. It's weird for you.

LEE. It's weird for anyone.

MANDREW. Whatever, so then this other guy comes in. Here, you come in, pretend you're the other guy.

LEE. Okay, I just — ? *(Lee gets up and pretends to reenter.)*

MANDREW. Yeah, you come in and you're wearing a full space suit, but it's got a zipper in the back and you can zip the whole thing right off like a onesie.

LEE. Why am I wearing a space suit?

MANDREW. Uh, because we're in space?

LEE. Of course we are.

MANDREW. It's *Planet of the Tits.* The chicks are aliens, we're space dudes —

LEE. I thought what you're wearing was from the movie? You said you were wearing that to promote *Planet of the Tits* —

MANDREW. Yeah, there's more than one costume in the movie, Lee. It's basically a regular Hollywood, big-budget blockbuster movie that goes a little bit further with the sex.

LEE. Right, and how long did it take to shoot?

MANDREW. Six days with stunts. Now let's go, you come in, you rip off your space suit, and you start going down on the other chick —

LEE. Your cousin Amanda.

MANDREW. Not my cousin, the forbidden one, you start goin' down on her while I'm goin' down on the other one … *(Lee gets into his "going down" position, which looks kind of like he's looking under a car. Mandrew laughs.)* … and then all of a sudden we start fucking them, at the same time.

LEE. We just both start — ?

MANDREW. Yeah, like we just kind of slide up and in, like this … *(Mandrew demonstrates and encourages Lee to follow. They mime throughout the rest of the scene.)*

LEE. Okay …

MANDREW. Yeah, we're just fucking away, goin' thrust for thrust and then — and this is a Fingers idea — the two guys, we start making eye contact with each other.

LEE. Uh oh.

MANDREW. Yeah, and at first it's kind of like, "Yeah! Look what we're doin'! We're fuckin' these chicks in space, motherfucker!" And we start high-fiving …

LEE. Like — ?

MANDREW. Like, yeah, just high-fiving as we're fucking the chicks. It's like, fuck-five, fuck-five, fuck-five … *(Lee and Mandrew high-five each other as they go through the motions. Lee starts enjoying himself.)*

LEE. Okay, I think I got it!

MANDREW. But hold up, 'cause then it gets real serious.

LEE. Oh shit.

MANDREW. Yeah, like maybe we're not laughing about the fact that we're fucking these chicks anymore. Maybe we're just lockin' eyes, you know? Like in a real serious something's-taking-over-and-I-kind-of-want-to-see-where-it-goes kind of way. And the high-fives all of a sudden start getting slower. It's like fuck … five … say it with me now …

LEE and MANDREW. Fuck … *five* … fuck … *five* … fuck … *five* …

MANDREW. And then they're not even real high-fives anymore, it's like our hands are just brushing against each other, and then we lock.

LEE. We lock?

MANDREW. We lock hands like this. *(Mandrew grabs Lee's hand and holds it up in the air.)* And we're still fucking … *(More thrusts.)* … but we're connected, see? It's like one hand now. It's like the sound of one hand fucking. That's what the title should be. 'Cause it's like one guy, one body, fucking two chicks at once. You understand?

LEE. Yeah, it's really —

MANDREW. It's really beautiful, is what it is. I get emotional just thinking about it, and I didn't even cry in that Disney movie about the old man and the balloons. That's how powerful it is. And that's why I'm taking home the award tonight. Because of Fingers and his beautiful film, which you haven't had the chance to see. *(Mandrew tears off his wrap, revealing his incredible body as he changes into a tiger-print jacket and leather pants.)*

LEE. I promise, I will watch it, Mandrew, I just —

MANDREW. I just thought you might want to see my award-winning performance.

LEE. What if you don't win?

MANDREW. Okay, well first of all that's a redundant question because I will win tonight —

LEE. It's not a redundant question —

MANDREW. *And secondly,* I don't think you appreciate the fact that I'm inviting you not just as a reporter, but as a friend, to share in my success, when in fact I don't have friends.

LEE. You don't have friends?

MANDREW. Okay, no — don't print that. I have *friends*, I just don't want friends, because a) if I want to fuck someone I can just go to work, and b) if I want companionship I've got a dog.

LEE. And a wife.

MANDREW. And a wife, and c) I don't trust these dudes, you know? These dudes who want to be friends now. I mean, you and me, we've got history. We were on Yearbook Committee. That's a special bond. We can go years without seeing each other, but we know each other, you know? I mean look at us! *(Mandrew stops in front of Lee, his genitals uncomfortably close to Lee's face.)* We're like finishing each other's ...

LEE. Sentences — ?

MANDREW. Sentences, bam.

LEE. I don't think I *do* know everything about you. I don't know how you got into the business ...

MANDREW. All right, I'll tell you for real. When I first moved out west, I was delivering sandwiches in the San Fernando Valley. And I kept having to go to these small production companies, like RCG Adult Video, and I thought, wow, I love getting sandwiches for people, but wouldn't it be awesome if I could *not?* If I could *not* do that, and actually do something else? I've never — I don't know if I'm like ADD, or ADHD, or just retarded, but I've never been able to sit back and watch other people doing shit without wanting to get up and do it myself. So I answered an ad for an adult film, and boom boom boom, here I am.

LEE. Okay, when you answered the ad, what happened? Did you ... audition?

MANDREW. Obviously.

LEE. And what did that consist of? Did you ... have sex with someone?

MANDREW. Well, I didn't prepare a monologue. *(Lee laughs.)* Why is that funny? I could monologue your ass off right now.

LEE. No, I know ...

MANDREW. *(Channeling Mo'Nique from* Precious.*)* "You sit there and you judge me, and you write them notes on your note-pad, because you think you know who I am ... "

LEE. What are you doing?

MANDREW. *(With building emotion.)* "But, those … those things she told you I did to her? Who else was going to love me? Who else was going to touch me?!"

LEE. Is this from *Precious* — ?

MANDREW. "WHO ELSE WAS GONNA MAKE ME FEEL GOOD ABOUT MYSELF?!"

LEE. Mandrew!

MANDREW. What?

LEE. Why are you doing Mo'Nique from *Precious*?

MANDREW. Because it fits! You're sitting there with your note-pad …

LEE. But why are you doing a monologue? Why are you doing a black woman's monologue?

MANDREW. Because you laughed at me when I said I didn't prepare a monologue!

LEE. No, I laughed because I could never do that. I could never have sex in front of a bunch of people like that, so I'm just interested in what it's like to sleep with all those … performers.

MANDREW. Look, I don't want to exaggerate? It's probably the most difficult thing in the world. And that's why, when you get famous like me and you win an award that says you're the best, all these people are like, "Whoa. I didn't even know you were the best. But now I do. And I want to party with you." You should come to the party!

LEE. What?

MANDREW. You should come with me, after the show! It's gonna be the sickest party in Vegas on the biggest night of the year other than Christmas.

LEE. Oh, I don't know.

MANDREW. I'm talking pools, hot tubs, beautiful naked ladies, boom boom boom, fucking ice sculptures, topiary, celebrities like … feeding each other grapes and … pizza bagels.

LEE. It sounds like fun. But I'm here with someone, so.

MANDREW. Who are you here with?

LEE. My fiancée. I finally got engaged. *(Beat. Mandrew mimes explosions coming out of his head.)* What are you doing?

MANDREW. My head is exploding! You're engaged?

LEE. See, this is why I didn't tell you —

MANDREW. You're *engaged?* If it's Sara Meyers …

LEE. I'm engaged to Sara Meyers. *(More explosions!)* Please stop exploding!

MANDREW. I knew it! I knew it in high school! I knew it was … *(Singing.) Love, love, love … this man is in love, love, love …*

LEE. That's not a song —

MANDREW. You guys must love each other so much.

LEE. We do.

MANDREW. Yeah. You guys must "love" each other so much —

LEE. Aw, come on, man …

MANDREW. What? You come on, buddy …

LEE. We have a very satisfying sex life. We do all the — all kinds of the sex things, that everyone does —

MANDREW. Like what?

LEE. Like crazy, sexual things.

MANDREW. Like?

LEE. Like … sex in the bathroom. We just had sex in the bathroom, so —

MANDREW. Just now?

LEE. No.

MANDREW. On the plane?

LEE. No.

MANDREW. In the airport? In the dirty public airport bathroom?

LEE. No, in our bathroom at home, before we left. I mean, technically the bathroom's *off* our bedroom and we actually ended up in the bedroom, but —

MANDREW. Bo-ring!

LEE. You know what? I knew as I was saying that, that you were going to react like that, but the thing that you don't understand is that Sara and I are actually pretty crazy and wild, and it's not just about sex for us. We take day trips all the time, so —

MANDREW. You take *day trips?*

LEE. Can we finish the interview? I'm supposed to be interviewing *you*. This is business.

MANDREW. The business of fucking.

LEE. Mandrew!

MANDREW. Can I fuck Sara?

LEE. No. What kind of question is that? You're *married*.

MANDREW. So what? I fuck other chicks all the time.

LEE. Yeah, on film.

MANDREW. So I'll film it.

LEE. Okay, and your wife would be cool with that?

MANDREW. I don't want to talk about my wife!

LEE. You guys have been having problems?

MANDREW. *I'm* not having problems. She's the one acting like a dinosaur.

LEE. What do you mean?

MANDREW. What do you think I mean? She's literally acting like a dinosaur. She's been seeing this shrink, who's got her doing this primal therapy thing, and she screams like a dinosaur whenever she gets pissed. *(From the hallway, we hear a primal, guttural ...)*

PEEPS. *(Offstage.)* ROAAAAAAAAR!

MANDREW. There she is. You might want to stand back ...

LEE. What? *(Peeps bursts through the door. Heavy makeup. Leather boots.)*

PEEPS. ROAR!

MANDREW. Baby —

PEEPS. ROAR!

MANDREW. BABY!

LEE. If this is a bad time ...

PEEPS. *(To Lee.)* How could Sundown do this to me?!

LEE. Sundown LeMay?

PEEPS. Yes, Sundown LeMay, after everything I've done for her, she doesn't even tell me?

LEE. What did she do?

PEEPS. She got new tits! She's parading around the lobby with Chuck Wood, with her fuckin' pepperoni nipples poking through the material like a couple of eyeballs, looking at me, *judging* me 'cause I don't have big tits, I don't even have titties, I just have these like little cow teets ... I have no idea who you are, by the way.

MANDREW. Baby, this is Lee, my friend from high school. Lee, this is Peeps, short for Pussy Boots.

LEE. Pleasure to meet you —

PEEPS. Do you like my tits, Lee?

LEE. What? No. I mean — I've never even seen them, so —

PEEPS. Because they're so small! I got a couple of baby tits. Which is good, 'cause I do barely legal shit, like schoolgirls and babysitters and shit like that, but if Sundown LeMay's doin' the same thing with these super-size tater tats, where the fuck does that leave me?

LEE. I'm sorry, are you asking me — ?

PEEPS. I'm asking you, Lee.

LEE. I don't know. I think a lot of guys don't even pay attention to that kind of thing.

PEEPS. Well thank you for lying, but it's the fucking *betrayal* that gets me more than anything. That that bitch would go behind my back and not even *tell* me. She did her first girl-on-girl with me. We're like *sisters.*

LEE. You've got history.

PEEPS. Exactly!

MANDREW. Look, baby, if you want to get big tits, you can get big tits.

PEEPS. I don't *want* big tits, you fucking deaf person! The second you get big tits, everything changes. Instead of a schoolgirl, you're the schoolteacher, instead of the slutty young secretary, you're the slutty *old* secretary. And next thing you know? You're a MILF. Which is fine, when you're like *forty.* I'd be perfectly happy to be the hot mom, fucking all the neighbors' kids. That's like … a dream of mine.

LEE. Right, so a "MILF" is a "Mom I'd Like to Fuck" …

PEEPS. WHY ARE YOU WRITING THAT?!

MANDREW. I told you, baby, he's doing an interview with me for the *New York Times.*

LEE. Actually —

PEEPS. The TV show?

MANDREW. It's not a TV show, baby, it's a big newspaper.

PEEPS. I know what it is! I was makin' a joke, you fucking taint-faced fuck!

MANDREW. *Okay,* baby! Calm down, okay? It's a big night for all of us. I'm just gonna put that in the *stratosphere* …

PEEPS. You're so smart, baby.

MANDREW. Don't interrupt, baby.

PEEPS. I bought him a word-a-day calendar.

MANDREW. That's not where that's from. I learned that on my own, so don't —

PEEPS. No you didn't. It was yesterday's word, "stratosphere" —

MANDREW. *Can I speak?* It's a big night for all of us, I'm just gonna put that … out there. And there is nowhere that I would rather be than right here with my best friend …

LEE. We haven't seen each other in a long time.

MANDREW. And my beautiful wife.

PEEPS. Aw, baby …

MANDREW. So let's go to the awards, and celebrate at the party.

LEE. I don't think I can come to the party. Sara will be waiting for me.

PEEPS. What? You have to come! It'll be so much fun.

LEE. I know, but Sara —

MANDREW. Lee. This is the biggest night of my life. It's basically the biggest night of anyone's life. And you're the only one who's known me since the beginning. I need you by my side.

PEEPS. You've got history.

LEE. I'll … okay, I can come for a bit.

PEEPS. YAY!

MANDREW. *That's* what I'm talking about! Two friends … driven apart by distance and time, yet coming together for one magic night.

LEE. All right — *(Mandrew hugs Lee from behind.)*

MANDREW. Can you feel how excited I am? *(Lee's eyes widen in horror.)*

LEE. Yes.

Scene 2

Lee's hotel room. The same as Mandrew's but reversed. (Is this symbolic? You bet your ass it is!)

Lee's fiancée Sara sings a song like Barry Manilow's "Can't Smile Without You" as she gets ready for the evening.* Lee emerges from the bathroom, also getting ready.

LEE. Hey darling, you're not going to sing Barry Manilow after this weekend, are you?

SARA. I might. I might sing Barry Manilow forever. Is that going to be a problem?

LEE. I don't know if I can marry a Fanilow …

SARA. Ah, you're just jealous because you're not going to the concert. I'm so excited for tonight!

LEE. Yeah, you and Mandrew. Both very excited.

---

* See Special Note on Songs and Recordings on copyright page.

SARA. Oh my God, you're actually calling him "Mandrew" now?

LEE. Yeah, well, he takes the whole thing pretty seriously.

SARA. What, the porn star awards?

LEE. Actually, they prefer to call themselves adult performers.

SARA. You know, I was looking through your little awards catalogue…?

LEE. Don't read that … *(She picks up the catalogue.)*

SARA. And I just don't know which of these "serious" films is going to win tonight. Will it be *Spontaneass*? Or maybe *Cum on My Bum*? Or will it be … *I Ate Chinese and Now I'm Hungry Again*?

LEE. Okay —

SARA. It's not too late to join me for Barry Manilow, Lee. It could be like a honeymoon before the honeymoon, we could do the whole Vegas thing, we could go see a magic show and gamble inside of a pyramid …

LEE. Sara, I have to go to the awards. It's for work.

SARA. All right, well … as long as we get to have fun after.

LEE. Oh … I might have to do something after the awards, so.

SARA. What?

LEE. I might have to do something with Mandrew. Your concert's probably going pretty late, so —

SARA. What do you have to do with Mandrew?

LEE. There's this party with the performers. I'd invite you, but it's not really your thing.

SARA. How is it not my thing?

LEE. Oh, you know, it's just a casual party for people who happen to be very comfortable with their bodies.

SARA. Well, I'm sure you'll fit right in, Lee. Since you can't even go swimming without a T-shirt.

LEE. Okay, first of all, it's not a T-shirt, it's a *wet* shirt.

SARA. Yeah, a wet T-shirt.

LEE. And secondly, I am wiiiide open sexually, okay? Unlike you, I don't hide under the covers to read my little sexy novels every night.

SARA. Sexy novels? What are you talking about? What sexy novels — ?

LEE. Like that one you were just reading about the girl who's getting it on with her boss and he's getting it on with someone else?

SARA. *Jane Eyre?* I'm sure that does seem like a sexy novel to you, Lee. I know what your fantasies are like.

LEE. What does that mean?

SARA. Remember when we tried to role-play? What did you want me to be?

LEE. *(Mumbles.)* Schoolteacher.

SARA. A schoolteacher.

LEE. A lot of guys fantasize about schoolteachers!

SARA. I *am* a schoolteacher! You couldn't even think of another thing!

LEE. So what? Is it such a bad thing that I want *you?*

SARA. No, it's sweet. But I have trouble reconciling *that* Lee with the Lee who wants to go to a party with a bunch of porn stars and get friggin' … water-boarded or something.

LEE. Well, I — what?

SARA. You know, when they put their boobs in your face.

LEE. Motor boating?

SARA. Yeah, whatever.

LEE. It's not *water boarding.* It's not a torture technique.

SARA. Okay, I'm sorry I don't know all the terms. Jesus, it's amazing you think you're such a sex expert, just because you've watched a few pornos.

LEE. Yeah, well it's amazing I didn't get into porn sooner, considering I've been having sex with the same woman my whole life. *(Lee starts to laugh … until he sees Sara's face.)*

SARA. That's really funny.

LEE. Sara, come on. It was a joke! We were both joking.

SARA. Yeah, I got it. You want to go to a porn party because you find me boring.

LEE. I didn't say that —

SARA. You make it sound like I'm not enough for you.

LEE. I was joking!

SARA. Do you think I'm enough for you?

LEE. *Yes. (Beat.)* But —

SARA. *But?*

LEE. But we're in Vegas. You can't blame me for being intrigued by Mandrew's lifestyle.

SARA. Uh, yes I can. You think I don't get bored, Lee?

LEE. No. What?

SARA. This may surprise you, but my ultimate fantasy growing up didn't involve rubbing Vick's VapoRub on my fiancé's chest every night.

LEE. I have seasonal allergies! You said you didn't mind.

SARA. I don't! I don't mind being an old married couple, but we'
not married yet, and we are getting older. Everyone else is marrie
the friggin' porn stars are married —
LEE. The wedding's a month away!
SARA. I'm so thrilled!
LEE. You're not thrilled?
SARA. Of course I'm thrilled that you finally put a ring on it, but
all you've done is cover this little bit of space on my finger and now
I've got this great big hole in my heart because it's clearly freaking
you out and I'm worried —
LEE. That you won't be enough for me? Sara —
SARA. No, that you won't be enough for *me. (Lee is stunned. Sara
turns for the door.)*
LEE. Sara, where are you going?
SARA. I'm in Vegas, Lee. I think I'll be *Spontaneass. (She exits,
slamming the door.)*

Scene 3

Mandrew and Peeps' hotel room. Same time.

*Mandrew wears his tiger-print suit, while Peeps stands in
front of him in a Juicy tracksuit, holding a hairbrush like a
microphone and clutching cue cards in her hands.*

PEEPS. Baby, I can't do this!
MANDREW. Don't freak out, baby. It'll all be on the teleprompter.
PEEPS. But it goes too fast! In rehearsal it kept moving.
MANDREW. So that's why we're practicing. Try it again from
the top.
PEEPS. Okay, so I go, "Pussy Boots: We're here to present the
award for Best Male Performer. Sundown LeMay: For all the guys
out there, this is the *biggest* award of the night ... "
MANDREW. Baby ...
PEEPS. What?
MANDREW. You don't have to read your names out loud. Just

read what you say.

PEEPS. I know that. What do you think I am, a fuckin' moron?

MANDREW. Okay, sorry.

PEEPS. *(Beat.)* I don't even read my name? 'Cause they gotta know who I am.

MANDREW. Someone's gonna announce you.

PEEPS. Fine, but if they don't announce me, I'm sayin' it.

MANDREW. Start again. *(Peeps starts again, reading the names under her breath this time:)*

PEEPS. So. "We're here to present the award for Best Male Performer." Sundown: "For all the guys out there, this is the *biggest* award of the night." Me: "Speaking of *biggest,* all of these performers are endowed with huge talent." Sundown: "*And* cocks." Don't you think I should say that line?

MANDREW. No, baby, you have to say the lines they give you.

PEEPS. But that bitch gets the biggest laugh!

MANDREW. Yeah, but the way you say your lines is funnier.

PEEPS. I can't believe I have to present with that whore.

MANDREW. Just read the nominees, baby.

PEEPS. I don't read the nominees. They get some British woman to do a voiceover so we don't fuck up the names. She's like ... *(Bad British accent.)* "Mandrew Rod-Dick ... Chuck Woooood ... "

MANDREW. Chuck Wood. Motherfucker's like ninety years old. He's not gonna win.

PEEPS. I didn't say he was.

MANDREW. So just read the winner.

PEEPS. But I don't know the winner.

MANDREW. Baby ...

PEEPS. Okay. "And the award for Best Male Performer goes to ... Mandrew Rod-Dick!" Yay! *(Peeps claps. Mandrew acts surprised and gets out of his chair. He stops when he realizes Peeps isn't watching.)*

MANDREW. Baby?

PEEPS. Yeah?

MANDREW. You're not looking. You have to watch my reaction.

PEEPS. Oh, sorry. I thought we were practicing for me.

MANDREW. We're practicing for both of us. Does it look like I'm surprised? Or does it look like "here we go again?" *(Mandrew sits down and gets up again, throwing his hands up and mouthing "Here we go again.")*

PEEPS. It looks like "here we go again."

MANDREW. Good.

PEEPS. You're saying "here we go again" with your mouth.

MANDREW. I'm not saying it —

PEEPS. You're mouthing it.

MANDREW. Well don't look at my mouth. Look at my hands, is it like —

PEEPS. It's like "here we go again."

MANDREW. Good.

PEEPS. But you've never won before.

MANDREW. So?

PEEPS. So why are you saying "here we go again" if you've never won?

MANDREW. Well, I *will* have. This is my *year*, okay? I can feel it in my dick.

PEEPS. I just don't want you to be disappointed.

MANDREW. I *won't* be disappointed. Ever. About anything. I'm taking Best Actor, Best Couples Scene …

PEEPS. With me.

MANDREW. Yeah. So here, I win, I come up …

PEEPS. You give me a kiss …

MANDREW. I give you a kiss …

PEEPS. Don't kiss Sundown!

MANDREW. What? What if she tries to kiss me?

PEEPS. Don't kiss her, baby! I'll kill you.

MANDREW. What am I supposed to do?

PEEPS. Slap her in the tits.

MANDREW. I'm not gonna slap her in the tits. She was in the movie with me. I have to thank her.

PEEPS. I *know* she was in the movie! But guess who *wasn't* in the movie? Me! Because Fingers never asked me. And he's never *gonna* ask me unless I get big jugs and if *I* get big jugs I'm gonna have to be a MILF in everything for forever.

MANDREW. Well, baby, if you're working with Fingers, you know it's gonna be beautiful.

PEEPS. That's easy for you to say. You're gonna be like Chuck Wood and still fucking any girl you want when you're fifty. When I'm *thirty* I'll be doing grandma porn and getting a fucking Lifetime Achievement award.

MANDREW. Hey, at least you've won awards. How do you think

I feel, watching you win all the time?

PEEPS. Are you even listening to me? I don't want to be a MILF.

MANDREW. I know, but —

PEEPS. I'm not ready to be a MILF!

MANDREW. I know, but —

PEEPS. I'm pregnant.

MANDREW. What?

PEEPS. I'm pregnant. With a baby.

MANDREW. Is it mine?

PEEPS. Yes, you fucking fuck.

MANDREW. Baby, you've fucked a lot of guys …

PEEPS. I've been careful. They always cum on my face.

MANDREW. And you're sure you're pregnant, like from a doctor?

PEEPS. Yes.

MANDREW. *(Beat.)* Well *that's* awesome!

PEEPS. You think so?

MANDREW. Uh, yeah! Don't you?

PEEPS. I don't know. I don't think I can work anymore. I don't want some random dude poking his dick into my baby.

MANDREW. Baby, there's no way you're working. I'll work double if I have to. Or I'll get another job, a real job. Or I'll direct! I picked up a lot from Fingers, I think I could do it.

PEEPS. Oh baby, this is cute.

MANDREW. It's awesome! I'm gonna be a dad! *(He kisses her.)* Wow. This really puts things in perspective, you know.

PEEPS. Yeah. What do you mean?

MANDREW. Well it's like, you have a baby and nothing else matters, you know?

PEEPS. Yeah. Like what?

MANDREW. Like I don't know … like if you kissed someone, or —

PEEPS. Who did you kiss?

MANDREW. I'm not saying I did, I'm saying if someone did …

PEEPS. Who the fuck did you kiss?

MANDREW. Sundown LeMay. *(Peeps paces around the room, looking for something.)* Baby …

PEEPS. I need a gun.

MANDREW. Baby, you don't need a gun.

PEEPS. I need to kill you. I need to kill you with something. *(She opens her suitcase, throwing clothing.)*

MANDREW. Baby, can I speak? Will you let me speak? *(Peeps spins around with a giant dildo in her hand.)*

PEEPS. Aha! Bend over, motherfucker.

MANDREW. What are you doing?!

PEEPS. I'm gonna fuck you in the asshole, you fucking asshole! *(She throws the dildo and he dodges it.)*

MANDREW. Baby, she was going through some shit! Her mom was in the hospital.

PEEPS. My mom's fucking *dead!* Where's my fucking kiss on the lips? *(Mandrew tries to kiss Peeps, but she pushes him away.)* No! Go away.

MANDREW. Baby —

PEEPS. I don't want to talk about this now. I'm too sad. I can't even roar.

MANDREW. Baby, you are totally overreacting! You never used to care about kisses.

PEEPS. Well things are fucking changing, okay? Put *that* on your *New York Times* show.

MANDREW. Baby —

PEEPS. I am a MILF now, okay? I am gonna be the MILF of your child. I am not Pussy Boots anymore, I'm like a Pussy … Woman. Okay? I'm changing, and if you don't wanna change with me? If you're gonna keep running around kissing every person with a sick mom in the world …

MANDREW. I can't change what I already did! What do you want me to do about it?

PEEPS. I want you to go. Please. Go away. *(Mandrew relents, moves towards the door, but stops.)*

MANDREW. What about the red carpet? I don't want to go by myself.

PEEPS. I don't give a shit.

MANDREW. Are you at least gonna sit with me? I don't want to be by myself when they call me up.

PEEPS. They're not going to call you up. You didn't win.

MANDREW. You don't know that.

PEEPS. I looked in the envelope.

MANDREW. You'd better be lying …

PEEPS. I'm not —

MANDREW. You'd better be lying, Peeps, 'cause I don't even care if I win. But I would hate to think that you'd deliberately ruin a surface.

PEEPS. You ruined my surprise. You ruined my pregnant surprise.

MANDREW. *(Softer.)* What about Best Couple?

PEEPS. We're not gonna win.

MANDREW. You looked in that envelope, too?

PEEPS. No. That one I just know.

Scene 4

A bar in the hotel lobby. Just before the awards.

Sara sits alone at the bar, checking her phone.

Chuck Wood enters. A veteran performer with a happy-go-lucky attitude. Sundown LeMay is on his arm. High heels and brand-new cleavage.

CHUCK. Hey, whose asshole do I have to fist to get a drink around here? Am I right? *(Noticing Sara.)* Pardon me, madame. I did not know there was a lady present. The name's Chuck Wood, and this beautiful creature on my arm is Miss Sundown LeMay.

SUNDOWN. They call me Sundown because I *go* down. *(Whispers.)* Like the sun.

CHUCK. Sundown's working on her porno speak. I've been acting as her mentor.

SARA. I actually know who you are.

CHUCK. You *do?* Don't tell me you're a fan! Don't tell me you've seen all my work …

SARA. No, I saw you on *Celebrity Boxing?* You lost to that little person?

CHUCK. They call them *midgets* now, dear, and that was but a minor valley between the voluptuous peaks of my career. But I'm back now, and when I win the big one tonight? My comeback will be complete. Emphasis on "cum," emphasis on "back." Whose back? Maybe yours if you're lucky.

SUNDOWN. I'm the luckiest girl in town!

CHUCK. *(Sits with Sara.)* You know what I like about you, Princess?

SARA. You can call me Sara.

CHUCK. Princess Sara, you are a real woman. I can see that. No fake tits for you.

SARA. That's what *I* always say.

CHUCK. I'm from the era of saggy tits and hairy bushes and natural curves …

SUNDOWN. Let's talk about something else.

CHUCK. I look at you and I see what every guy *really* wants.

SARA. A high-school teacher with a big student loan?

CHUCK. Absolutely. Money doesn't matter. I grew up in the San Fernando Valley, in the seventies, you think we cared about money?

SUNDOWN. No.

CHUCK. It was the Garden of Eden, baby — full of innocence and hardcore fucking. I didn't even know I was being *filmed!* I was just fucking, and I'm talking twosomes, threesomes, foursomes, more-somes, gang-bangs just for kicks and ice packs on our dicks. I would fuck anything, and no one ever got anything, except money, which literally turned into coke in our hands. And no one ever died. That was the amazing thing, no one ever died.

SARA. That can't be right.

CHUCK. Well, I don't remember. I was full of drugs.

SUNDOWN. Let's! Do! Drugs!

CHUCK. Sundown …

SUNDOWN. Sorry.

CHUCK. But the after-parties were out of this world! In 1979, we had the greatest pie-eating contest on the roof of Caesar's Palace. Except instead of eating pies? We ate assholes.

SARA. *(Horrified.)* Oh my God, that's not a pie-eating contest at all. I should go, I've got a date with a famous singer …

CHUCK. It's been a pleasure meeting you, Princess. You truly are the complete package, and if you're interested, I'd like to offer you *my* complete package.

SARA. Well, that is tempting, but … *(Sara stops, as Lee enters behind Chuck.)* I'd like to hear more about this package.

CHUCK. Thatta girl!

SUNDOWN. What do you want to know?

SARA. Is it … all-inclusive?

CHUCK. More like all-intrusive. *(They laugh, together, flirtatiously.*

Lee is confused.)
LEE. Sara?
SARA. *(Overenthusiastic.)* Oh, *hi,* Lee! I didn't even see you there!
CHUCK. This must be the famous singer …
SUNDOWN. Sing something!
SARA. Actually, this is my fiancé, Lee. He's a journalist.
CHUCK. Well come on over and join the fun, Neil!
SARA. Chuck was just telling me about his penis.
SUNDOWN. Yeah. That was a *deep* conversation.
CHUCK. Very good! *(They all laugh.)*
LEE. Can we just wait a minute?
SARA. What's the matter, Lee? We're not boring you, are we? I know how easily you get *bored.*
LEE. Can we talk in private?
SARA. We can talk about *Chuck's* privates. Oh my God, I just did one! *(Chuck and Sundown cheer.)* Maybe you can mentor *me* next, Chuck …
CHUCK. Bingo! I love these open relationships.
LEE. *(Uncomfortable.)* Right, but joking aside …
SARA. Lee is "wide open, sexually."
SUNDOWN. You can interview me if you want. In my *mouth.*
LEE. Okay, we're all having fun, but —
CHUCK. We're about to have a *lot* of fun.
MANDREW. *(Entering.)* Chuck! Leave her alone.
SARA. It's all right, *Man*drew …
MANDREW. Sara, I don't have time for a big reunion right now, okay? The awards are gonna start any minute —
SARA. I wasn't —
SUNDOWN. Good luck tonight, Mandrew! *(She tries to kiss him, but he blocks her.)*
MANDREW. No! I don't have time for that. I'm already way behind schedule. In case you didn't hear, Chuck, I'm doing an interview with the *New York Times.* I think it's the centerfold, so …
CHUCK. I already met your friends, Mandrew. They're joining me for the awards.
LEE. Wait, Sara's not coming to the awards.
SARA. Why not?
CHUCK. You can sit with me, in the *front row.*
MANDREW. Oh, they put you in the front because you're too old to see the stage.

CHUCK. I sit in the front because I need extra legroom … for my cock!

SARA. Why can't I come, Lee? You never even asked me.

LEE. I didn't think you'd want to come.

SARA. You didn't give me the choice!

MANDREW. Let's go, Lee.

LEE. I just thought I'd feel embarrassed if you were there.

SARA. *Embarrassed?*

LEE. No, I mean *I* would be …

SARA. Yeah, I got it. Chuck, let's blow this joint.

LEE. Sara —

CHUCK. Yeah, and if you're lucky I'll let you blow my joint!

SARA. *(Laughs, flirtatiously.)* Oh my God, you're terrible. *(They walk off together, leaving Lee stunned.)*

MANDREW. This is not good.

LEE. I know.

MANDREW. I was supposed to do the red carpet before Chuck.

SUNDOWN. I was Chuck's date.

MANDREW. So let's go! Are you coming or not, Lee?

SUNDOWN. Oh, he's coming, all right. I mean … *(In Lee's face.)* He *will* be.

MANDREW. Can we please just go?

LEE. I don't know what's happening.

SUNDOWN. Semen! *(In an explosion of lights and music, we transition into …)*

Scene 5

The Adult Film Awards. We hear …

BRITISH WOMAN. *(Voiceover.)* Ladies and gentlemen, welcome to the Adult Film Awards. Tonight we honor the best adult entertainers of the year with the awards for the best adult entertainers of the year awards. So sit back, relax and enjoy the show. *(The lights, music, and fireball sound effects reach a crescendo, then become muted, as we find ourselves … backstage, with Peeps and Sundown.*

Extravagant dresses, heavily made up. Tension in the air. Peeps looks at Sundown's enormous new breasts, then away.)

PEEPS. How's your mom doing?

SUNDOWN. She's in remission.

PEEPS. She's in *Michigan?*

SUNDOWN. No. What?

PEEPS. What did you say?

SUNDOWN. I said my mom's getting better.

PEEPS. Perfect.

SUNDOWN. What do you mean "perfect" — ?

PEEPS. I mean that's perfect. *(Peeps glares at Sundown for a moment ...)*

SUNDOWN. Why are you looking at me? *(... and then lunges at her, and starts aggressively making out with her. Peeps pulls away.)*

PEEPS. You're not even good.

SUNDOWN. I don't even know what's going on!

PEEPS. You're a shitty kisser. That's what's going on.

SUNDOWN. That's not what you said when we did *Twelve Angry Lesbians.*

PEEPS. It's called acting. Just like you've been acting like we're friends all these years.

SUNDOWN. Peeps, I honestly don't know what you're *talking* about. *(Peeps takes out her phone.)*

PEEPS. That's weird ...

SUNDOWN. What?

PEEPS. My phone still works. But for some reason you didn't call me to tell me you were getting new tits, you FUCKING WHORE!

SUNDOWN. I didn't know!

PEEPS. What do you *mean* you didn't know?

SUNDOWN. I'm not a planner, okay? Sometimes life just happens.

PEEPS. And you just do whatever you want, don't you?

SUNDOWN. Peeps! Please!

PEEPS. Please what?!

SUNDOWN. Please don't say mysterious things! I don't know what you're talking about!

PEEPS. I'm talking about Mandrew, you whore! How could you do this to me? Get up in my stratosphere?

SUNDOWN. What do you mean? You said it was okay if I worked with him.

PEEPS. Yeah, I said you could *work* with him, I didn't say you could go crying to him about your sick mom and then kiss him on the lips!

SUNDOWN. Oh. Yeah.

PEEPS. *(Mocking.)* "Oh, yeah." You fucking kissed him and now I can't get this image outta my head —   .

SUNDOWN. It was one time!

PEEPS. It was one time too many, bitch. It's fucking over.

SUNDOWN. Good, I fucking hate you.

PEEPS. I fucking hate you, too.

BRITISH WOMAN. *(Voiceover.)* Ladies and gentlemen, Pussy Boots and Sundown LeMay. *(Peeps and Sundown put on their best smiles, walk onstage, into the spotlight, up to the podium. They read off the teleprompter, stilted and monotone.)*

PEEPS. "Pussy Boots good evening. We're here to present the award for Best Male Performer."

SUNDOWN. "For all the guys out there, this is the biggest award of the night."

PEEPS. "Speaking of *biggest,* all these performers are endowed with huge talent AND COCKS!"

SUNDOWN. What the fuck? That's my line!

PEEPS. And the nominees are! *(As the announcer takes over, Peeps and Sundown wrestle. Peeps slaps Sundown's breasts. Sundown pulls Peeps' hair. Projections of the nominees appear overhead.)*

BRITISH WOMAN. *(Voiceover.)* The nominees for Male Performer of the Year are … Blade Buttler, Little John Big Dong, Antonio Bonederass, Black Attack, Mandrew Rod-Dick, and Chuck Wood. *(Sundown pins Peeps, but Peeps pushes her off.)*

PEEPS. That's our cue! Get off me, bitch!

SUNDOWN. You punch like a girl.

PEEPS. You punch like a whore! *(Peeps grabs the envelope, tearing it open.)* And the award goes to … oh my God, this is a surprise …

CHUCK WOOD! *(Spotlight on Chuck in the audience. Total shock. He bounds towards the stage, blowing kisses to his fans. He accepts the award, kissing both girls, then addresses the audience from the podium.)*

CHUCK. Oh boy, I promised Black Attack I wouldn't cry, but … I was not expecting this. *(Composing himself.)* When I was a boy, I told my father that I was going to be the first Jew in the Basketball Hall of Fame, or a famous rock star, like Neil Diamond or Barry Manilow. My father looked at me and said, "Good for you, son, but some people don't give a shit about basketball. Some people don't even listen to music." I know I don't. *Pointless.* "But," he said, "there's one thing you can count on. One thing that unites every human being on this planet and it's this: Everybody fucks. So if you're the best at fucking … you're the best human being." *(Beat.)* I did not understand these words at the time — I was only six — but when I made my first adult film in 1978, I thought of my father. Not at the time of shooting, of course, but in a general sense. The film was *Bad News Boner.* For my bone-tastic performance, I was awarded the Best New-Comer trophy, but sadly, my father died one week before the ceremony. I was devastated. I didn't know where to turn. I didn't understand that the answer was right in front of me. *(Looking out.)* It was you. My fellow performers. You've opened your hearts and your legs to me, and while I keep giving it to you, you keep giving *everything* to me. So Papa, if you can hear me up there, I want you to know this: I may be the best human being. I may be the best at fucking. But I'd be nothing without all the people that I've fucked. *(Holds up his award.)* Thank you, have a wonderful night!

Scene 6

A bar in the hotel lobby. Just after the awards.

Mandrew talks on his cell.

MANDREW. *(Into phone.)* I'm fine. Yes, I am. Trust me, everything is fine. It's not rigged. People just didn't vote for me! I don't know! Because they didn't! I'm not yelling, Mom. *(Lee enters, drinks in hand.)* Okay, I have to go, I'll call you later. *(Really quiet.)* I love you, too. *(Hangs up, macho.)* Sorry. That was my agent.
LEE. Your mom is your agent?
MANDREW. Okay, it was my mom! So what? She's the one who calls *me* every day. "When are you sending me another film?" "When are you coming home?"
LEE. You send her your films?
MANDREW. I cut out all the sex. She likes the acting. What kind

of drinks are those?

LEE. White Russians?

MANDREW. White Russians? What are you, a millionaire? *(Mandrew takes his, begrudgingly, and drinks it fast as Lee checks his phone, nervously.)* What are you doing?

LEE. Did you see where Sara went? I lost her after the awards.

MANDREW. I don't know. She's probably at the party or something.

LEE. Are we going to the party?

MANDREW. Why? So you can talk to Chuck Wood?

LEE. No, but if Sara's there —

MANDREW. I'm sorry, are you writing an article on Sara now?

LEE. No, but —

MANDREW. Here's a headline for you: "Guy Who Was Supposed to be My Friend Cares More About His Fiancée Than He Does About Me."

LEE. Mandrew ...

MANDREW. I can't believe I was considering making you a godfather to my baby.

LEE. What baby?

MANDREW. The baby that Peeps is having!

LEE. I didn't even know that she was pregnant?

MANDREW. Neither did I! And it's turning her into a crazy person! She always said I could fuck whoever I want and then she gets pregnant and pulls a bait and whatever on me.

LEE. Bait and switch.

MANDREW. I know what it's called, Lee! I did a movie called *Bait and Switch,* except "Bait" was spelled B-A-T-E and it was about a guy who switches bodies when he masturbates.

LEE. That's ridiculous.

MANDREW. It *is* ridiculous! She acts like she's so cool about everything and then we get married and I *kiss* one girl and she freaks out! *(Mandrew takes Lee's drink and downs it.)*

LEE. I don't understand why you'd kiss *anyone* when you already sleep with girls for a living.

MANDREW. I don't understand a lot of things, Lee.

LEE. *(Beat.)* All right.

MANDREW. Remember those nights we spent working on the yearbook together? Eating pizza bagels, shooting the shit ...

LEE. That was fun.

MANDREW. It was *very* fun. Remember you put like a hundred pictures of Sara in the yearbook?

LEE. Yeah, not transparent at all.

MANDREW. You always knew what you wanted, and you got it. Sometimes I wish that you and me could switch bodies through masturbation.

LEE. Well, that's a nice thought, but I think most guys would rather be a … performer than a …

MANDREW. Civilian …

LEE. Yeah, a "civilian" like me, who's only slept with one person.

MANDREW. What do you mean "one person"? Like at a time?

LEE. No, in my life. *(Mandrew's head explodes.)* Please stop doing that! You know that Sara and I got together in high school.

MANDREW. That is awesome!

LEE. It's not awesome.

MANDREW. Okay, can I speak for a second, Lee? Can I speak?

LEE. No one's … interrupting you —

MANDREW. I'm about to lay a truth on you, okay? If I had to choose between fucking just Peeps for the rest of my life and every other chick I've fucked combined? I'd choose Peeps, nine times out of ten. And the tenth time? I'd regret it.

LEE. *(Sincerely.)* I think I made a big mistake with Sara.

MANDREW. Well, best friend, you know what?

LEE. We're just regular friends.

MANDREW. I can help you. I've still got my yearbook and you know what it says under my name? "Most Likely to Succeed."

LEE. Did you write that in there?

MANDREW. I *did* write that in there.

LEE. You really think you can help me? *(Mandrew smiles and throws his arm around Lee.)*

MANDREW. I *know* I think I can help you.

Scene 7

Lee and Sara's hotel room. Same time. Sara enters and collapses on the bed.

A knock at the door. She answers it, revealing Peeps, who looks like hell from the fight.

PEEPS. Hi, can I use your bathroom? My room's down the hall but the toilet's busted and I'm pregnant too I'm Peeps by the way.

SARA. I know who you are. You're pregnant?

PEEPS. I know who you are, too! I saw you at the awards. You're not going to the party?

SARA. Um, no. I think I've seen enough for tonight, so —

PEEPS. Do you mind if I go to the bathroom? If you're just gonna talk about yourself for a while?

SARA. Sure. I wasn't, but go ahead.

PEEPS. Thanks. I am kinda pissin' for two right now. I mean, I don't know if that's a thing, but if I got a baby in there, and it's alive, something tells me it's gotta piss. I'm not a scientist.

SARA. I could call the front desk about your toilet, or — *(Peeps leaves the door open as she uses the bathroom.)* Oh. Let me just close that for you …

PEEPS. *(Offstage.)* Hey, I'm not embarrassed. Even the fuckin' Queen has to piss sometimes. I think it must be so funny, when the Queen has to take a shit? She's all like, "Ooh, I'm the Queen, let's have a tea party in my palace and then I'll take a little shit."

SARA. Yeah. We can talk after, if you want.

PEEPS. *(Offstage.)* Mandrew says I shouldn't flush, because of the environment, but it's not my room, so. *(The toilet flushes. We hear Peeps washing up.)*

SARA. I love that he's "Mandrew" now. In high school, we just called him —

PEEPS. *(Rushing out of the bathroom.)* No, don't tell me don't tell me! He doesn't want me to know.

SARA. Oh, sorry …

PEEPS. No, it's fine, it's just — that's Mandrew. He likes to keep secrets. *(Peeps lies down on the floor.)*
SARA. I'm not … completely sure what I'm supposed to do right now?
PEEPS. He's cheating on me.
SARA. Okay. Well, that's terrible.
PEEPS. Yeah, and then the bitch that he kissed *hits* me. Fuckin' unprovoked, I might add.
SARA. This is the woman he slept with? Or he just kissed her?
PEEPS. UGH! You're just like my porn friends.
SARA. I don't think *that's* true.
PEEPS. You're in a real relationship, too, you're supposed to get it. Why do you think I wanted to talk to you? Why do you think I pretended my toilet was busted?
SARA. Your toilet isn't broken?
PEEPS. No, that was a trick so I could talk to you.
SARA. Seems unnecessary …
PEEPS. I bet *you've* never been cheated on.
SARA. Well … I kind of have.
PEEPS. What do you mean "kind of"? Just the tip?
SARA. No … I mean, this is really embarrassing, but I was like eight, and my neighbor Sean went for ice cream with another girl, and at the time I thought —
PEEPS. This is already not the same.
SARA. I know it's not the same. But feeling betrayed is feeling betrayed. When I was eight —
PEEPS. You liked ice cream, I get it. But Mandrew kissed my best friend when we have a rule about no kissing because we need one thing that's just for us.
SARA. Right. But how can you have a rule about kissing when you're having sex with other people for a living? Can you even *have* sex without kissing? I mean, I know you can, I know what sex is, obviously, but — look — I think it's great that you're try-ing to have a monogamous relationship, in some way. I think it's great that you're trying to have kids together, and trying to make it work —
PEEPS. I'm not *trying* to have kids, I'm fucking having one, and I know you think I can't do it, 'cause I'm in porn —
SARA. I don't think that, I'm just trying to understand. And I really don't know anything about porn. I mean, I read a paper in

grad school, but …

PEEPS. I read that paper, too, but let me tell you something: I *can* fucking do it. I can get clothes and feed her, and take her to school. I already thought, you know … this is so gay, I'm such a fuckin' whore, but I was telling Mandrew how the first thing I'd do if I got a baby is get one a those picture frames that says "First Day of School." You know, for when it's her first day of school? You can get those frames that already got it written on there, and I could take a picture with her in her little backpack and put it in the frame, and then we'd know that it was her first day of school. I mean, that's fucking gay, but …

SARA. I don't think you're using that word correctly …

PEEPS. But I just thought that was one thing I could do.

SARA. So it's a she?

PEEPS. I don't fuckin' know. Does it matter?

SARA. No, sorry.

PEEPS. Whatever it is, it's goin' to school and I'm gonna take a picture of it. You know … I had a teacher. When I was like ten I had a teacher, Mr. Rob, and he always took pictures of me. You know, like naked pictures?

SARA. What?

PEEPS. No, I'm fuckin' with you. He never molested me.

SARA. Oh. Good one.

PEEPS. *(Laughs.)* Yeah. *(Peeps stares at Sara.)* Does anyone ever tell you that you've got a smile like a summer's day? I mean, I'm not lezzing out or anything. You just seem like the kind of person who people would go, "Hey, you've got a smile like a summer's day."

SARA. Lee says things *like* that.

PEEPS. I bet he does. I bet he says all kinds of romantic shit. I bet you do it in a bed, on your back, with fuckin' candles everywhere and the window drapes blowing, and you listen to Enya music and kiss each other's lips and hold each other until you fall asleep.

SARA. Well, yeah. I mean, not exactly like that, but we can be romantic.

PEEPS. I bet you think I'm gross. I bet you think this whole thing's gross.

SARA. I don't think you're gross.

PEEPS. Why did you leave the awards?

SARA. I left because … I was bored.

PEEPS. You were bored?

SARA. I mean, it wasn't all boring, the part where you presented was not boring, but I just couldn't get into it. I mean, I don't know if I thought it would be sexy, or that I'd actually get turned on or something, but I don't find it exciting. And I'm not threatened by it. I know that Lee and I have a great sex life. We've been practicing for a really long time.

PEEPS. That's the best.

SARA. I don't think Lee actually wants to sleep with a porn star, but now I don't know *what* he wants. And at this point, that's scary. Because if he's losing confidence, it makes me lose confidence, too. And I don't know, is he right to think that we're missing something? *(Beat.)* That's not a rhetorical question.

PEEPS. No, that's a good question.

SARA. I mean, why do you do porn? You must get something out of sleeping with all these different people, right?

PEEPS. Oh, I get money. They pay me for it.

SARA. No, I know, but do you get something like … emotional, or … I don't know, experiential … that you wouldn't get if you didn't sleep with all those people? Because I heard this thing. You know *This American Life*?

PEEPS. Man, do I ever.

SARA. I mean the radio show, on NPR?

PEEPS. Oh *that* American life, yeah.

SARA. I heard this thing that your body gives off these endorphins during sex which aren't related to like … the actual physical stimulation, but to whether or not you feel safe, and secure, and loved. So I just wonder if it's better for you at home, with Mandrew, because you have that closeness?

PEEPS. Ugh, when me and Mandrew get together … it's like the gods are fucking.

SARA. Great. But do you know that it's better because you've been with other people?

PEEPS. It's like this: You know the movie *Freaky Friday*?

SARA. Yeah, I love that movie.

PEEPS. I love that movie too!

SARA. Yay! Okay …

PEEPS. Yay, so I was telling someone about it and they were like, oh, have you seen the original? And I was like original *what*? Because I'd only seen the Lindsay Lohan version, you know, back when she was super cute —

SARA. Sure —

PEEPS. So then I went and watched the original and I was like what the fuck is this? Who's this fucking boy-girl and why is she waterskiing?

SARA. Jodie Foster.

PEEPS. And then I went *back* and watched my version again, and I loved it even *more* because I was so glad that it wasn't like that other piece of shit. You know what I mean?

SARA. I do. But I already know which version I like. I like *my* version, *my* original. And maybe it's not always going to be thrilling, but I don't know if you can avoid that.

PEEPS. Maybe you can! Maybe you just have to surprise each other. One time, Mandrew had to go to Germany to shoot a movie called *Das Booty*?

SARA. Okay —

PEEPS. And I was like great, I'll come with you, I love Germany. But the truth is, I don't like Germany at all, ever since World War Two. I just said that because I knew he was doing this bondage scene with five sexy German chicks, so I put on a leather mask and a dominatrix costume and I snuck in and fucked him in a dungeon full of flames and then I whipped off my mask like Scooby Doo and I was like, guess what, it's fucking *me*, you just fucked your own wife, motherfucker! And he didn't even know! So.

SARA. *(Beat.)* I don't think that's going to work for me. And honestly, I'm not sure it really worked for *you*. Because basically, what I'm hearing is that you traveled all the way to Germany because you can't just tell Mandrew how you feel. It's okay to need something, Peeps. I need someone who's going to love me when it's not surprising. I need someone who loves me even when it's boring. Because it will be, sometimes. Sometimes you can't have sex in a German dungeon, sometimes you have to be an old married couple, rubbing Vick's VapoRub on each other. But that can be amazing, too.

PEEPS. I wish you were just like a TV show and I could have you on all the time. You and Lee, you're so perfect, you're so smart …

SARA. We're not perfect. I don't want to be perfect. I would like to be a little more fun and spontaneass. I would like to be able to pull off a dress like that.

PEEPS. So take off your clothes. *(Peeps begins to strip.)*
SARA. What? What are you doing?
PEEPS. Isn't it obvious? We need to switch bodies, like *Freaky Friday*! You wear my dress and I'll wear yours! I'll be the normal nerdy chick, and you'll be the super sexy performer!
SARA. Why?
PEEPS. Because! It's fun. And it's something we can do.
SARA. *(Considers.)* Are we even the same size?
PEEPS. Strip! Strip! Strip! Strip!
SARA. Pass me the dress. *(Sara exits to the bathroom. Peeps follows.)*
PEEPS. Oh my god, you're being ridiculous.
SARA. *(Offstage.)* You're coming in with me?
PEEPS. *(Offstage.)* You've already seen me piss. Now take this off.
SARA. *(Offstage.)* I've been meaning to buy new underwear.
PEEPS. *(Offstage.)* That's okay. Check this out.
SARA. *(Offstage. Beat.)* Oh.
PEEPS. *(Offstage.)* No underwear!
SARA. *(Offstage.)* Yeah, no … nothing down there.
PEEPS. *(Offstage.)* Holy fuck, that looks so hot on you.
SARA. *(Offstage.)* Really? I don't know if it … fits …
PEEPS. *(Offstage.)* Wait, shut up, do you hear something? *(We hear the key card in the main door.)*
SARA. *(Offstage.)* Oh my God, shut the door! *(She pulls the bathroom door shut just as Mandrew enters through the main door with Lee, who is blindfolded.)*
MANDREW. All right, are you ready for your surprise?
LEE. I don't understand why I have to be blindfolded.
MANDREW. Don't question it. You can take off the blindfold … now.
LEE. Okay, it's my hotel room. What was the point of that?
MANDREW. What did I just say? Don't question it.
LEE. Sara's bag is here …
MANDREW. Lee! Forget about Sara! Sara's at the party with Chuck right now, having the time of her life. And if Sara were here, you know what she'd say? Sara would say, I want Lee to be happy. And what's the one thing that will make you happy, Lee? Say it with me now …
LEE. Making … Sara … happy.
MANDREW. *(Overlapping.)* Sex … with a … porn star.
LEE. What? *(Mandrew throws the door open, revealing Sundown.)*

SUNDOWN. Ta da! *(Sundown hums a bit of "Ghostbusters" as she backs in …)*

LEE. Wait, what's going on?

MANDREW. You said that being a porn star was every man's fantasy, did you not?

LEE. No —

MANDREW. You said you've only slept with one person and you made a big mistake.

LEE. Those were separate thoughts —

MANDREW. There's no need to thank me, Lee. Just say —

SUNDOWN. You're welcome. *(She kisses Lee just as Sara comes out of the bathroom.)*

SARA. Lee? *(She's wearing Peeps' sparkling dress. It's a poor fit, but she looks transformed.)*

MANDREW. Holy shit.

SARA. What are you doing with her?

LEE. Nothing! It was Mandrew's idea!

MANDREW. It was supposed to be like earlier, with the two chicks, fuckin' side-by-side, fuck-five —

SARA. What is he talking about?! You were fucking chicks earlier?

LEE. No! I was just faking it, with Mandrew —

MANDREW. It's from my movie, it was a reenactment —

LEE. *(At the same time.)* It was a reenactment.

SARA. *(Re. Sundown.)* And what about *her?* Were you doing a "reenactment" with her, too?

SUNDOWN. Is this the other chick?

SARA. What other chick?

SUNDOWN. He said there'd be another chick. *(Peeps bursts out of the bathroom, in Sara's clothes.)*

PEEPS. I'M the other chick, bitch!

MANDREW. Baby!

PEEPS. ROAR!

LEE. What is going on?!

MANDREW. You were hiding in the bathroom?!

PEEPS. *(Sarcastically.)* No, I was taking a shit. What am I, the Queen of fucking England?

SARA. I never thought you'd do something like this.

LEE. I didn't! I'm sorry, I told Mandrew I made a big mistake —

SARA. I made a big mistake, too.

LEE. Sara —

SARA. Don't follow me. *(She exits. Peeps follows her.)*

PEEPS. I'm gonna follow her because *she's* my new friend and *she's* not a fuckin' homewrecker.

SUNDOWN. I didn't know. He said there was another chick …

PEEPS. You wanna know who the other chick is? She's standing right there … *(Points at Lee.)* And she's a chick with a dick, and balls, and she's a guy, and he's a dick, and so is he, and so are you, and I fucking hate all of you, and I'm fucking pregnant! *(She exits, slamming the door. Silence.)*

SUNDOWN. You know, there's a party on the roof …

MANDREW. Sundown? I think I need some time alone with my friend.

SUNDOWN. Okay. Are you talking about me? Or…?

MANDREW. I'm talking about Lee.

LEE. I'm not your friend.

MANDREW. You just said you were. You said we were regular friends.

LEE. She was the girl that you kissed, wasn't she? And you told her there'd be another chick? Who was the other chick? Your pregnant wife? Someone else?

MANDREW. I hadn't thought that far ahead.

LEE. Do you think at all, Mandrew? Do you think about anything, ever?

MANDREW. Hey, this is not my fault. I was trying to help you —

LEE. It's *completely* your fault! You invited me up here, you tried to get me to cheat, to be like you, and now Sara thinks that we were having sex with two girls earlier —

MANDREW. Well I didn't know she was hiding in the bathroom looking sexy as fuck, did I?

LEE. That's not the point! I don't live in the same world as you, where you can run around having sex with all these random people, and it's okay, as long as it's on film and as long as you don't kiss them, and there's all these stupid rules, I mean —

MANDREW. I wanted to impress you, okay? I just wanted to impress you!

LEE. You wanted to impress *me?* You're gonna be a father, Mandrew.

MANDREW. I know.

LEE. So what's your kid going to think when he finds out you're a porn star? *(Beat. This hits Mandrew harder than Lee intended. He immediately regrets it, but the damage is already done.)*

LEE. Mandrew — *(But he's gone. Lee takes out his phone, frantic.)*

SUNDOWN. Don't you hate the splits? *(We suddenly realize that Sundown is still there. She slides into the splits.)* I hate how easy they are. I hate how easy it is to do the splits.

LEE. Sundown. My fiancée is *gone.*

SUNDOWN. Oh. I'm sorry. *(Comes out of the splits.)* She died?

LEE. YOU WERE STANDING RIGHT THERE!

SUNDOWN. Oh, the chick with the ring!

LEE. Yes! I need to go after her.

SUNDOWN. You don't know where she is! She said not to follow her.

LEE. Fine, then I'll wait for her. But you need to go.

SUNDOWN. Do you want to play "Chicken"?

LEE. No.

SUNDOWN. It's really fun! I try to touch your dick, and when I get too close you go, "CHICKEN!"

LEE. Sundown, no, you need to get out of here. If she comes back —

SUNDOWN. She's not coming back! Hello, even I can see that. *(Lee sits on the bed, dejected. Sundown sits with him.)* You're not the only one with problems, you know. Do you have any idea what kind of shenanigans these gigantic boobs have gotten me into? I lost my best friend because of these boobs. And I don't think my mom's gonna like them.

LEE. Your mom doesn't know?

SUNDOWN. No. I was thinking I could wait until Halloween to see her, and wear a big costume to cover them up? I could just see her on Halloween every year.

LEE. Maybe. *(They smile.)*

SUNDOWN. Have you seen my movies?

LEE. Yeah. I did some research.

SUNDOWN. Have you ever fantasized about me?

LEE. No. And even if I did, it's one thing to fantasize and it's another thing to meet someone in the … flesh. It would be like Mandrew meeting Waldo from *Where's Waldo.* Except that would never happen because —

SUNDOWN. He's so hard to find.

LEE. Yeah. And, you know … not real.

SUNDOWN. But I'm real. Everything about me is real, except for my giant fake titties. And you can have me. I wouldn't tell anyone.

How many guys can say they've had the P.S.E.?

LEE. What's the P.S.E.?

SUNDOWN. Porn Star Experience. Do you even know how good I am?

LEE. I can imagine. But I just … can't.

SUNDOWN. *(Beat.)* Mandrew was right about you.

LEE. What did he say? That I'm a tight-ass or something?

SUNDOWN. No. He said you're a good person. *(Sundown places her hand on Lee's knee. He looks at it.)*

LEE. I'm not a good person, Sundown. I'm just … *(She reaches for his crotch. He stops her.)* Chicken.

Scene 8

The bar in the hotel lobby. Same time. Chuck sits alone with his award, talking into a tape recorder.

CHUCK. I had a scare once. About … five, ten years ago. I woke up and found a gelatinous, cheeselike substance on the base of my balls. Could've been any number of diseases. Turns out it was cheese. I'd been eating a panini naked, and I fell asleep as the cheddar dripped down onto my testicles.

MANDREW. *(Entering.)* Chuck?

CHUCK. Mandrew! I was just working on my memoir. *(Shuts off the tape.)* Doing a little dick-tation, no pun intended …

MANDREW. You intended that.

CHUCK. What are you doing here? I thought you'd be at the party on the roof?

MANDREW. I thought *you* would be.

CHUCK. I was, but I had to get out of there. It was so lame. You kids, you don't know how to have fun, you know? You're so serious. Everything's so clean and sterile. In my day, it was dirty, dirty, dirty.

MANDREW. Congratulations. On the award.

CHUCK. Well, I earned it.

MANDREW. Yeah, well, a lot of people worked pretty hard this year.

CHUCK. But I worked the hardest.

MANDREW. Some might say.

CHUCK. Most people would. I got the most votes.

MANDREW. Yeah, but … what are votes, you know?

CHUCK. Just the way you find out who's the best.

MANDREW. Yeah, well … who is the best, you know?

CHUCK. I am.

MANDREW. You know what? You're such an overrated hack —

CHUCK. You couldn't fuck your way out of a shopping bag —

MANDREW. Fuck you —

CHUCK. Fuck you —

MANDREW. Fuck you! *(Mandrew starts to exit.)*

CHUCK. Mandrew! *(Sweetly.)* Sit with me a minute. I'll let you touch it.

MANDREW. What?

CHUCK. The award.

MANDREW. You think I give a shit about your award? *(Mandrew sits with Chuck and touches the award.)* You think it's real gold?

CHUCK. I don't think so, no.

MANDREW. Probably not. It's probably like … silver or something.

CHUCK. All that glitters is not gold.

MANDREW. That's pretty true. *(Beat.)* Do you like White Russians?

CHUCK. Sure. I like White Russians, I like Black Russians, I like half-Russians …

MANDREW. I just got into White Russians, but I'm thinking of quitting. I'm having a baby.

CHUCK. I *heard* that you were pregnant.

MANDREW. Peeps is.

CHUCK. And yet here you are, sitting in an empty bar, feeling sorry for yourself.

MANDREW. *You're* here.

CHUCK. You want to compare yourself to me?

MANDREW. Why not? You're basically a living legend. You just won the biggest award on the face of the earth.

CHUCK. Let me tell you something, kid. Nobody wants to get laid because of who they *were. (Takes out tape recorder.)* Possible chapter title: "Nobody wants to get laid" — what did I just say? "Nobody gets laid … "

MANDREW. "Nobody … who gets laid … "

CHUCK. "Nobody … "
MANDREW. "Everybody …"
CHUCK. "Every legend …"
MANDREW. " … tells a story."
CHUCK. Not even close. *(Shuts off tape.)* This book is a disaster.
MANDREW. I'm sorry.
CHUCK. I was like you once. I was young and dumb, the world was my glory hole. I thought I could have it all. I thought I could have a relationship, maybe even a family … and still run around smooching my co-stars.
MANDREW. Sounds like someone I know.
CHUCK. I just said, I'm comparing myself to you.
MANDREW. Oh, right, okay —
CHUCK. You can't do whatever you want all the time.
MANDREW. But what did I do? It was one kiss, it didn't even matter to me —
CHUCK. It doesn't matter if it matters to you. It matters to her. I don't care if you're a porn star or whatever it is that other people do for a living. If love is involved, there's always a compromise.
MANDREW. I don't know. I look at you, and it seems like you have it all.
CHUCK. What have I got that you don't?
MANDREW. Respect?
CHUCK. Respect? You want to talk about respect? I got kicked out of a party tonight.
MANDREW. I thought you left?
CHUCK. I left because they kicked me out.
MANDREW. What did you do?
CHUCK. It's not important what I did.
MANDREW. What did you do?
CHUCK. I put my penis in a cake.
MANDREW. Why?
CHUCK. I'll tell you why. Because I'm standing there, at this fancy party, with my fancy award, and no one's giving me the time of day. So I think, I know what I'll do: I'll stick my penis in the cake. In the seventies, that shit killed. But instead of laughing, the ladies started screaming, I got pushed away, and all I could hear was this voice: "Whose gray pubes are in my angel food cake?" "Whose gray pubes." I heard that, and you know what my first instinct was? I started looking around, thinking I'd find the person with the gray

pubes. But it was me. They were my gray pubes. I was the very culprit I was looking for. And it had never even occurred to me that they were gray.

MANDREW. I'm sorry.

CHUCK. I used to be everyone's favorite joker. Now, I'm everyone's favorite joke.

MANDREW. What about Sundown?

CHUCK. Sundown's a child. You all are. And you've been very kind to an old man, giving me this award. I thought it meant that I could still do this. I hoped it was your way of saying welcome back. But now I know … it's a way to say goodbye. And I don't want to go. *(Chuck touches Mandrew's hand.)* I've got nothing else, Mandrew. But I look at you and I think, there's someone who's still got time to do it right. But you've gotta do it now. Before your pubes turn gray.

MANDREW. *(Moved.)* Talking like this, Chuck? I feel like you could be my dad.

CHUCK. *(Smiles.)* Given the life I've had? It's possible that I am.

Scene 9

Mandrew and Peeps' hotel room. Later.

*Sara is alone, sitting on the bed, drinking vodka from the bottle as she sings a song like "Can't Smile Without You," sadly … * A knock at the door. Sara stumbles over to open it, revealing Chuck.*

CHUCK. Pizza delivery.

SARA. Mr. Wood …

CHUCK. Do I have the wrong room? I was looking for Mandrew, or Peeps?

SARA. Mandrew isn't here. And Peeps went to get something.

CHUCK. Oh, okay. Well, thank you for accompanying me earlier, and sorry to bother you —

---

* See Special Note on Songs and Recordings on copyright page.

SARA. Maybe I want to be bothered. *(Chuck stops.)*

CHUCK. Pardon?

SARA. I'm all alone … in Vegas … with the *biggest* porn star in the world … maybe I want to find out what the big deal is. *(Sara tries to lean against the wall, seductively, but slips, and Chuck catches her, taking the bottle.)*

CHUCK. Oh boy, have we had something to drink tonight?

SARA. What are you, a cop? This is America! *(Pursuing him.)* I don't drink. I'm too much of a lady. Have you ever wondered what it's like to be with a lady, Mr. Wood? A *real* lady? *(She plays with her hair until it completely covers her face.)*

CHUCK. Sweetheart, I see what's going on here …

SARA. Uh oh, where'd I go? Just a bunch of hair over here.

CHUCK. That's very cute.

SARA. Peek-a-boo. Just me under this hair. But maybe you'd rather see the hair … down there. *(She points to her crotch.)*

CHUCK. Under normal circumstances, that might have appealed to me …

SARA. HEY! Come here. I got a secret.

CHUCK. Sweetheart —

SARA. *(Chasing him.)* Come here! You've got a big penis?

CHUCK. *(Stops.)* Yes I do.

SARA. Guess what. Guess what.

CHUCK. What?

SARA. *(Loud whisper.)* I've got a big vagina.

CHUCK. Okay, I think we need to work on the pillow talk.

SARA. Or maybe we shouldn't talk at *all.* Maybe we should do it.

CHUCK. No, no, no, you don't even know me. You think I can teach you something and of course I could, but you don't want to have sex with *me.*

SARA. I want to have sex with you like every five minutes. You know how many times that is? I do, I'm a math teacher. That's twelve times an hour, sixty times in five hours …

CHUCK. That sounds exhausting.

SARA. Not for me. I'm a fucking dynamo, man. I just need to sit down for a second. *(She collapses face-down on the bed.)*

CHUCK. Oh dear …

SARA. Oh yeah. You like that? You like me like this? Do you want this so bad? *(She wiggles her bum.)*

CHUCK. Why don't we get you some coffee …

SARA. Yeah, get me some coffee, bitch! I want you to get me some coffee and pour it all over my face — oh my God, what am I saying?! *(She bursts into tears.)*

CHUCK. Oh dear, oh sweetheart.

SARA. This isn't me, Chuck!

CHUCK. I know, I know. Here, have some water. *(He passes her water. She drinks, spilling everywhere.)*

SARA. I just want to be me, and be okay with it, and have everyone else be okay with it.

CHUCK. I know.

SARA. I don't want to *Freaky Friday.*

CHUCK. I know. I don't know what the hell you're talking about, but I know.

PEEPS. *(Offstage. From the hallway.)* RrrrrrooooooaaaaaRRRRRRR!

CHUCK. What's happening? *(A key card is swiped. Peeps bursts through the door.)*

PEEPS. Roar!

SARA. Peeps! Did you get it?

PEEPS. It's on Pay-Per-View! Fingers told me! *(Peeps grabs the remote and sets up the Pay-Per-View.)*

CHUCK. What's on Pay-Per-View?

PEEPS. Mandrew's movie. What are *you* doing here?

CHUCK. I was looking for Mandrew. I wanted to make sure he followed through on something.

PEEPS. Well good. You can watch his movie and tell me if he's got a thing for Sundown.

CHUCK. What movie? *Planet of the Tits?*

PEEPS. Yes, obviously.

CHUCK. You know, I was in that movie.

PEEPS. I know you were in the movie! Every single person was in the movie! Now just watch his scene with Sundown and tell me what you think! *(They all watch the screen and we hear …)*

MANDREW. *(Voiceover.)* This isn't right! You can't keep me captive! Tied in these chains like a slave …

SUNDOWN. *(Voiceover.)* Too bad for you, Colonel George Dicklor. But there's only one way off this planet.

MANDREW. *(Voiceover.)* You mean…?

SUNDOWN. *(Voiceover.)* That's right. You're gonna have to fuck your way off.

SARA. Uh oh.

CHUCK. You've gotta be kidding me.

PEEPS. What?

CHUCK. You're actually threatened by this? I've never seen such a passionless scene in my life.

PEEPS. What do you mean?

CHUCK. Look at him, arching his back so she can't lick his face. And look at the positions — doggy-style, reverse cowgirl? He might as well have been doing a crossword.

SARA. He *seems* pretty into it.

CHUCK. Of course he does. That's how good he is.

PEEPS. You think he's a good actor?

CHUCK. You want the God's honest truth? I think he's the second-best I've ever seen. But you know what requires *no* acting? His scenes with you.

PEEPS. Oh shut up, what do you mean?

CHUCK. There's love in your scenes. Sustained eye contact … French kissing … the way he aims his cumshot so it doesn't hit your eyes? You guys are gonna be great parents. *(A knock at the door. Peeps pauses the movie.)*

PEEPS. That might be Mandrew.

SARA. Or it might be Lee. *(Chuck opens the door. Sundown enters, with an award.)*

SUNDOWN. I've been in the hallway for like fifteen minutes, you were supposed to get me.

PEEPS. What are *you* doing here?

SUNDOWN. I just wanted to say! That I'm sorry I got new tits without telling you, and I'm also sorry … that we're not friends anymore, Peeps. Because I miss you, and winning Best Anal wasn't the same when you weren't there to share it with me. So I want you to have this.

PEEPS. You want me to have your Best Anal?

SUNDOWN. You deserve it. You deserve all of life's happiness. You deserve the best. Anal.

PEEPS. You're right. I do deserve Best Anal. Because I've been acting like a great big asshole. *(She hugs Sundown, taking the trophy.)*

SUNDOWN. Are you really keeping the award?

PEEPS. Yeah. *(Another knock. Sara opens the door, revealing Lee.)*

LEE. Hey. I was looking for Mandrew.

PEEPS. Everyone's looking for Mandrew.

LEE. Because I thought he might know where you were. And I wanted to talk to you. I kind of thought I'd get to talk to you alone, but —

CHUCK. We're not even here.

SARA. There's nothing to talk about, Lee. You want to explore your crazy sexuality ... I like Barry Manilow. You were with Sundown, I was with Chuck. Whatever.

LEE. What? No, I wasn't with Sundown.

CHUCK. She wasn't with Chuck.

LEE. When you left and Sundown started doing the splits —

SARA. I don't want to hear this ...

SUNDOWN. Nothing happened —

LEE. Nothing happened because I didn't want it to happen. When it was right there in front of me and Sundown was saying how many guys get the Porn Star Experience, I realized ... how many guys get the Sara experience? How many guys are lucky enough to marry a woman like you? Because that's what I want.

SARA. But how do you know? How do you know that you're not going to like ... want something else? How do you know we're not going to have regrets and resent each other forever?

LEE. I don't. All I know is that ... *(Sings a song like "Can't Smile Without You."*)*

SARA. Lee ...

CHUCK. It's a little flat, Neil.

SARA. You know the words.

LEE. I got us two tickets for the concert tomorrow night. You skipped it because of me, and I want to make it up to you.

SARA. But you hate Barry Manilow.

LEE. I do. I do hate him very much. But I really love you. And I want to give you the Barry Manilow Experience. *(A knock at the door. Peeps' eyes light up.)*

PEEPS. If this is Barry Manilow ... *(Chuck opens the door for Mandrew, who's holding a shopping bag.)*

MANDREW. Great, everyone's here. Thanks for the invitation.

CHUCK. I was looking for you.

LEE. I was actually in the middle of something with Sara ...

MANDREW. I think it can wait, Lee. I'd like to apologize to my wife, if you don't mind.

LEE. I was just apologizing to Sara —

MANDREW. Can you *not* steal my thunder? Is that possible? Could I have a little thunder to myself?

* See Special Note on Songs and Recordings on copyright page.

SARA. *(Taking Lee's hand.)* It's all right, Lee —

MANDREW. Sara! I don't need your help!

PEEPS. Just do it!

MANDREW. Fine! When we were talking about babies, you said you wanted a picture frame, and this one says "Happy Graduation," 'cause they didn't have "First Day of School," but I thought, you know, if I can't get first day of school I'll get the last day and it's basically the same shit. So there you go. *(He hands Peeps a picture frame.)*

PEEPS. Thank you.

MANDREW. I was a Boy-drew and now I'm a Mandrew. And the new Mandrew is going to make you feel like the special lady that you are, and the new Mandrew's not gonna cheat on you ever, and the new Mandrew doesn't keep any secrets, which is why I gotta tell you something.

PEEPS. If you fuckin' kissed someone …

MANDREW. My name isn't Mandrew. *(Sundown gasps.)* I changed it, to make it sexy.

SARA. Yeah, when I heard you were going by "Mandrew," I was like —

MANDREW. *Can I speak?* I've never told anyone this …

PEEPS. Baby, it's okay if you don't want to talk about it.

MANDREW. No, I want to tell you. But you can't laugh. You have to promise …

PEEPS. I won't laugh, I promise. Tell me your name, baby.

MANDREW. Okay. My real name is … Andrew.

PEEPS. *(Laughs.)* What the fuck?

MANDREW. You said you wouldn't laugh!

PEEPS. Okay, baby, I'm sorry. *(Peeps wraps her arms around Mandrew and they kiss.)*

LEE. Hey, Mandrew … I just wanted you to know … I am going to finish the article about you.

MANDREW. Is it still the centerfold?

LEE. That's not really a thing. *(Mandrew stares at him.)* All right, it's the centerfold.

MANDREW. Bam! That's what I'm talking about! *(Everyone celebrates.)*

LEE. I just want you to know that I'm your … fan. I'm a Fandrew.

MANDREW. Lee … how can you call yourself a Fandrew when you haven't seen my film?

LEE. Oh my God.

SARA. What's the big deal? We were just watching it.

LEE. You were just watching it?

MANDREW. I haven't even told you the ending, it's so beautiful. I'm riding a horse along the beach and I see the Statue of Liberty and I go … "The Statue? Which means … this is Earth! It was always Earth! This whole time I thought I was on the Planet of the Tits, but I was actually on Earth … all along."

SUNDOWN. That's the twist!

LEE. All right, I will watch it …

MANDREW. I don't want you to watch it, Lee. I want you to reenact it!

LEE. Oh please no.

PEEPS. Oh please yes!

MANDREW. Sundown! You can be the Statue of Liberty!

SUNDOWN. Can I be Sundown?

MANDREW. JUST BE THE STATUE OF LIBERTY!

PEEPS. *(With love.)* Look at him … directing.

MANDREW. Sara, you can be Sundown, and Lee, you be me, and Chuck … would you be my Dr. Zaius?

CHUCK. It would be an honor. *(Sundown grabs a "Where's Waldo?" book and the "Best Anal" trophy, which become her tablet and torch. Chuck stands above them on the bed, posing as Dr. Zaius.)*

LEE. I don't know what I'm supposed to do. *(Mandrew stands behind Lee and Peeps behind Sara, positioning them for the reenactment.)*

MANDREW. Just look at Sara and say, "What is it, Nova-gina?"

LEE. "What is it, Nova-gina?"

MANDREW. Good. Sara? *(Peeps whispers into Sara's ear and she repeats:)*

SARA. "I need you. My tits need you."

CHUCK. This chick's a natural.

LEE. *(Off Mandrew's whisper.)* "But I'm human. I'm flawed. Are you sure you'll need me forever?"

SARA. Can I think about it?

MANDREW. Sara —

CHUCK. "Stay away from him, Nova-gina! I need to lobotomize his brain!"

SARA. *(To Lee, off Peeps' cue.)* "It's not your *brain* I want. It's your … heart." *(The two couples come together in the most beautiful way possible as Mandrew recites the final lines of the movie:)*

MANDREW. "From this day forward, we will no longer call this the Planet of the Tits. We will call it … home. We will call it … "
CHUCK. " … the Planet of the Earth." *(Music swells. Lights swell. Everything swells.)*

End of Play

PROPERTY LIST

Notebook, pen
Catalogue
Hairbrush
Cue cards
Suitcase with clothing, dildo
Phone
Envelope
Award
Phone
2 drinks
Phone
Tape recorder
Bottle of vodka
Glass of water
TV, remote
Award
Shopping bag with picture frame

SOUND EFFECTS

Awards music
Applause
Toilet flushes